A Robbie Reader

ANDREW LUCK

Claire O'Neal

Mitchell Lane
PUBLISHERS
P.O. Box 196
Hockessin, Delaware 19707
Visit us on the web: www.mitchelllane.com
Comments? Email us: mitchelllane@mitchelllane.com

PUBLISHERS

Printing   1   2   3   4   5   6   7   8   9

A Robbie Reader Biography

Abigail Breslin	Drake Bell & Josh Peck	Miley Cyrus
Adrian Peterson	Dr. Seuss	Miranda Cosgrove
Albert Einstein	Dwayne "The Rock" Johnson	Philo Farnsworth
Albert Pujols	Dwyane Wade	Raven-Symoné
Aly and AJ	Dylan & Cole Sprouse	Robert Griffin III
Andrew Luck	Emily Osment	Roy Halladay
AnnaSophia Robb	Hilary Duff	Shaquille O'Neal
Ashley Tisdale	Jamie Lynn Spears	Story of Harley-Davidson
Brenda Song	Jennette McCurdy	Sue Bird
Brittany Murphy	Jesse McCartney	Syd Hoff
Buster Posey	Jimmie Johnson	Tiki Barber
Charles Schulz	Joe Flacco	Tim Lincecum
Chris Johnson	Jonas Brothers	Tom Brady
Cliff Lee	Keke Palmer	Tony Hawk
Dale Earnhardt Jr.	Larry Fitzgerald	Troy Polamalu
David Archuleta	LeBron James	Victor Cruz
Demi Lovato	Mia Hamm	Victoria Justice
Donovan McNabb	Miguel Cabrera	

Library of Congress Cataloging-in-Publication Data
O'Neal, Claire, author.
 Andrew Luck / by Claire O'Neal.
    pages cm. — (A Robbie reader)
 Includes bibliographical references and index.
 ISBN 978-1-61228-460-6 (library bound)
 1. Luck, Andrew, 1989– —Juvenile literature. 2. Football players—United States—Biography—Juvenile literature. I. Title.
 GV939.L81O64 2014
 796.332092—dc23
 [B]
                                                                    2013023052
eBook ISBN: 9781612285184

ABOUT THE AUTHOR: Claire O'Neal has written over two dozen books for Mitchell Lane Publishers. She holds degrees in English and Biology from Indiana University, and a PhD in Chemistry from the University of Washington. More importantly, Claire loves to root for the Colts, and not just because she was raised in Indianapolis and they are her hometown team. She currently lives in Delaware with her football-crazy husband and Eagles-fan sons. Claire dedicates this book in loving memory of her father, a raging Colts fan, who taught her everything she knows about football, including how much fun it can be to sit around and watch the game with your family.

TABLE OF CONTENTS

Words in **bold** type can be found in the glossary.

Andrew Luck (right) stands center-stage with his new Indianapolis Colts jersey. NFL Commissioner Roger Goodell had just announced that the Colts chose the young quarterback as the number-one pick in the 2012 NFL Draft.

Big Shoes to Fill

"With the first pick of the 2012 NFL **Draft**, the Indianapolis Colts select Andrew Luck, quarterback, Stanford."

The young man with thick brown hair stood up, flashing a broad grin. He hugged his family as his mom pinned a blue horseshoe to his suit. Andrew Luck stepped onto the stage of New York's Radio City Music Hall to loud cheers. NFL commissioner Roger Goodell held up a new blue football jersey with Luck's number, 12, shining in white. Stanford University's Luck officially became an Indianapolis Colt.

Luck joined a team that expected a lot from him. The Colts' star quarterback, the legendary Peyton Manning, had missed the entire 2011 season with a neck injury. While Manning healed, the Colts suffered through their worst season in 20 years with only 2 wins, and 14 losses. Colts owner Jim Irsay released Manning from the team on March 7, 2012, a move that angered many Colts fans. The people of Indianapolis adored their all-star quarterback. Manning was not just a legend on the field, but also a class-act who gave his time and money to children's **charities** in the Indianapolis area. As Luck himself told reporters in a press conference, "Peyton was my hero growing up."

Some people wondered how anyone, let alone a fresh-faced 22-year-old, could fill such big shoes. "'Big shoes' might be an understatement," Luck said at a news conference, "if I woke up every morning trying to compare myself to Peyton, I think I'd go crazy." But many football experts saw remarkable similarities between Luck and the future hall-of-famer Manning. Both have fathers who played quarterback in the NFL. Both led their college teams to award-winning seasons. Both were named runners-up for the Heisman Trophy, the nation's highest award in college football. Both were chosen as the number-one draft pick by the Indianapolis Colts, joining a losing team. Both are "football nerds"— smart and humble players who always strive to learn more about football.

Irsay saw all this, and more. He told *Indianapolis Monthly,* "It's not that often that you see organizations handing over the keys to a 22-year-old. You don't see it in the banking industry, the oil industry, or the computer business. But the level of maturity for Andrew is uncommon." Could Andrew Luck live up to the hype?

Luck celebrates his first win of the 2012 NFL season on September 16. The quarterback led the Colts to a 23-20 win at home against the Minnesota Vikings.

Ready to Play

Andrew Austen Luck was born on September 12, 1989, in Washington, DC, to dad Oliver and mom Kathy. Andrew got his football talent honestly. His dad played quarterback for West Virginia University, and then in the NFL with the Houston Oilers for four years. The Luck house loved football, but more than that, they loved learning. Even as he played in the NFL, Oliver continued his education in night school and in the off-season. He earned a law degree—to match the one that Kathy had.

When Andrew was just a year old, Oliver helped start the World League of American Football to bring NFL-style

The entire Luck family gathered to support Andrew at the 2012 NFL Draft. Left to right: sister Mary Ellen, mother Kathy, father Oliver, Andrew, brother Addison, and sister Emily.

action to fans overseas. Oliver managed the Frankfurt Galaxy and later the Rhein Fire, both in Germany. He then moved to London when he became president of the league. The Lucks joined him for a ten-year-long adventure in Europe. The close-knit family savored the history, culture, and scenery of Europe. They also welcomed Andrew's younger siblings, sisters Mary Ellen and Emily, and brother Addison.

When they weren't traveling, the Luck children enjoyed a typical childhood of school and sports. Andrew lived for soccer like many European kids. Even today his favorite athlete is American soccer player Clint Dempsey.

In 2000, Andrew's family moved to Houston, Texas. Fifth-grade Andrew was now ready for team football. He loved playing for the Lake Travis Wildcats, coached by his dad. Andrew knew even then that sometimes the most important lessons were learned from his mistakes. Once during practice in the Texas heat, Andrew felt dizzy and sick. His team needed him, but he had to sit on the bench . . . because he had forgotten to eat lunch! He told *Indianapolis Monthly*, "What's even more embarrassing is to be the kid sitting, watching practice, and you know nothing is wrong with you. I think that cuts a kid's pride." From then on, Andrew showed up prepared, for both practice and school, ready to handle whatever came his way.

Luck threw for over 7,000 yards and 53 touchdowns in his career as quarterback at Stratford High School in Houston, Texas.

Football "Nerd"

They say everything is bigger in Texas, and high school football is no exception. For a sophomore to play quarterback, and against some of the best teams in the state, is practically unheard of. But Andrew did just that at Houston's Stratford High.

Stratford Spartans Head Coach Eliot Allen said that Andrew wasn't just his best quarterback. Luck's speed, strength, and soccer-trained footwork also made him a great **safety**, punter, and field-goal kicker. In his sophomore year, Luck threw for 1,529 yards and 7 touchdowns. As a junior, he became a passing machine, with 2,926 yards and 27 touchdowns.

Meanwhile, Luck honed his skills as a double threat. Not many quarterbacks are big and fast enough to run the ball, but Andrew picked up around 700 rushing yards each year.

Andrew's true greatness lay in qualities that couldn't be measured. He describes himself as a "nerd" with a lifelong love of learning. High school teammate Marshall Hughes told *USA Today*, "He read a ton of books—several at a time." Andrew's quiet intelligence gave him focus and decision-making skills. In one famous pass during Stratford's **homecoming** game, Andrew's left shoe came off as a play began. He lost his right shoe wiggling away from a defender. Unfazed, Andrew ran, shoeless, to the far right

and tossed the ball high and long to receiver B.J. Griffin for a touchdown.

Andrew took his team to the playoffs his junior year, where they were the underdog in their first game against Cypress Falls High School. But Andrew showed his trademark cool under pressure. He threw 339 passing yards and four touchdowns in front of a huge audience at Reliant Stadium, home of the NFL's Houston Texans. Even though his team lost the game by one point, university scouts sat up and took notice of this promising young gun.

Andrew continued his high level of play in his senior year. He also studied hard, graduating from Stratford High in 2008 as class **valedictorian**. Colleges with huge football programs fought to offer him a full-ride **scholarship**—a free college education—to play on their teams. Andrew's choice would shock them all. He wanted to play for a losing team.

Luck's rushing skills give him an unusual edge. Here, Luck rushes for a touchdown in Stanford's win against the University of Washington on September 26, 2009. Luck rushed for almost 1,000 yards in his college career.

A Thinking Man's Game

The Stanford University Cardinal suffered through seven losing seasons of football. In 2006, they lost 11 out of 12 games. But Luck saw potential in the team, and in his new coach, former NFL quarterback Jim Harbaugh.

More importantly, Andrew wanted a great education. Stanford accepts only the best students, and Andrew fit right in. He told *Sporting News*, "People have way better things to worry about than who the quarterback of the football team is. There's a lot of brilliant people here." Andrew chose to study **architecture**, inspired by the European stadiums and historic buildings of his childhood. His talent

2011 Heisman finalists pose with college football's most prestigious trophy. Left to right, they are: Trent Richardson, Montee Ball, Tyrann Mathieu, Andrew Luck, and Robert Griffin III. Robert Griffin III won the award, but all five players earned a spot on an NFL team.

impressed Professor John Barton, who told *Sports Illustrated*, "He has a gift for seeing all these pieces at once, breaking them apart and putting them back together again. And I thought, 'That's what he can do on the field.'"

Andrew started his sophomore year in 2009 as Stanford's new quarterback. In this first year on the college field, Luck showed he was a football **prodigy**. His passer rating and yards per pass average were the best of any college quarterback in the Pacific-12 conference. His leadership took Stanford to the 2009 Sun **Bowl**.

Andrew's junior year was even better. College football showered Luck with honors—Heisman Trophy runner-up, All-American Team quarterback, and Pac-12 Offensive Player of the Year. He ended the season as the Orange Bowl MVP. NFL teams like the Carolina Panthers urged Andrew to quit school a year early to play professional football.

Playing a senior year at Stanford could put Andrew's football career at risk. What if he got hurt, or had a losing season? Andrew and his dad called the Manning family for advice. Peyton Manning had also been tempted to go pro after his junior year at the University of Tennessee. But Peyton chose to stay for one final year. Just before graduation, the Indianapolis Colts chose Peyton as their number-one draft pick.

Luck hands the ball to running back Stepfan Taylor (33) in a game against the Oregon Ducks on November 12, 2011. Luck's record-breaking senior season made him Stanford's all-time leader in career wins.

Luck huddles with his Stanford teammates just before the Tostitos Fiesta Bowl on January 2, 2012. Though the Cardinal barely lost a hard-fought battle to Oklahoma State in overtime, Luck won MVP honors.

Andrew chose to stay in school. He finished his college career with a 31-7 record in games he started, and he took the Cardinal to the 2012 Fiesta Bowl. But before Andrew could play professionally, he first had to walk . . . across the graduation stage. Stanford University gave Andrew his diploma on June 17, 2012, along with the Al Masters Award, the highest honor Stanford gives to a student-athlete.

Luck stands ready behind his Colts defensive line as they play to victory against the Kansas City Chiefs on December 23, 2012. Luck broke the record for most passing yards by an NFL rookie during this game.

ChuckStrong, LuckStrong

Luck came to Indianapolis ready to lead. His first pass in an NFL game was to running back Donald Brown for a 63-yard touchdown. Cornerback Jerraud Powers told the *Indianapolis Star*, "What gets me is for Luck to be so young as a **rookie** and his decision-making process . . . how he handles the game and how he thinks . . . that's what is going to make him better than people think." Colts owner Jim Irsay simply posted on Twitter: "Historic beginning . . . The legend has begun!"

With determination, teamwork, and a whole lot of "Luck," the 2012 Colts went on to inspire Indianapolis and the entire NFL.

Luck (wearing a red number 12 jersey) and the 2012 Indianapolis Colts pose for a team photo in November. Many Colts shaved their hair to support their coach, who lost his hair during his cancer treatment.

When Coach Chuck Pagliano battled cancer off the field, the Colts players shaved their heads in support, urging their town to be "ChuckStrong." On the field, Luck's offense got off to a slow start. At first, Luck struggled behind a young Colts defense. By the end of the season, Luck had been **sacked** 41 times, the fourth-most of any quarterback in the league. But the Colts also became the best in the NFL at second chances, turning third downs into first downs. Luck himself set an NFL record on November 4 in a win against the Miami Dolphins. He threw for 433 yards, the highest number ever for a rookie quarterback in a single game.

The Colts finished the season with 11 wins and a trip to the playoffs. Luck became the first number-one draft pick rookie quarterback ever to start a postseason game. Though the Colts lost to the Ravens, Luck had turned the team around. He didn't need to fill Peyton's big shoes. Andrew Luck had brought his own.

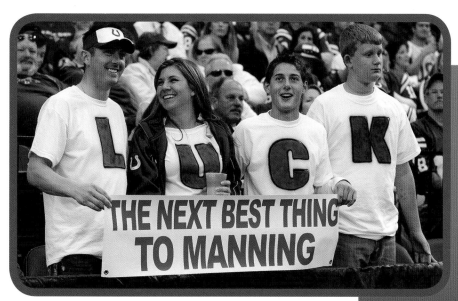

Colts fans suffered through a terrible 2011 season without Manning. Some hoped their bad 'luck' would bring them a talented new quarterback in the 2012 NFL draft.

Luck connected with running back Vick Ballard (33) to score a win in overtime against the Tennessee Titans on October 28, 2012.

Off the field, the new superstar just wants to be a regular guy. With a $22.1 million, four-year contract, Luck bought . . . a ping pong table. "My mom is really good," he tells interviewer Dave Calabro, but "my brother and I have surpassed her

Andrew Luck tells some young pals to 'go long!' Luck volunteers for Play 60, an organization that encourages kids to eat healthy and play outside for at least an hour a day.

now in ping pong skills." Luck also spends time at Indiana children's hospitals and other charity organizations. He encourages kids to stay fit and active with NFL Play 60. Indianapolis's new hero tells interviewer Nate Dunlevy, "I try to bring a smile to someone or positively impact the community in some way. It's the least someone in my position can do."

CAREER STATISTICS
College

Year	ATT	CMP	YDS	COMP %	YPA	LNG	TD	INT	SACK	RAT
2009	288	162	2,575	56.3	8.9	63	13	4	6	143.5
2010	372	263	3,338	70.7	9.0	81	32	8	6	170.2
2011	404	288	3,517	71.3	8.7	62	37	10	11	169.7

NFL

Year	ATT	CMP	YDS	COMP %	YPA	LNG	TD	INT	SACK	RAT
2012	627	339	4,374	54.1	7.0	70	23	18	41	76.5

ATT=Attempts; CMP=Completions; YDS=Yards; COMP%=Completion percentage;
YPA=Average yards per throw; LNG=Longest pass; TD=Touchdowns; INT=Interceptions;
SACK=Sacks; RAT=Quarterback rating

CHRONOLOGY

1989   Andrew Luck is born on September 12 in Washington, DC.

1990s   Luck family lives in Europe.

2000   Luck family moves to Houston.

2008   Graduates as co-valedictorian of Stratford High School in Houston, TX; begins college at Stanford University.

2009   Starts as quarterback in his first college game, throwing for 193 yards and 1 touchdown in a 39-13 win against Washington State University; misses Sun Bowl game due to a broken finger.

2010   Throws for 4 touchdowns and 316 yards in a 52-17 win against Sacramento State; rushes for college-career-high 92 yards in a 41-0 win against Washington.

2011   Named MVP in the first Orange Bowl ever played by Stanford University, a 40-12 win against Virginia Tech; sets Stanford record for most career touchdown passes (82), surpassing the previous record set by football legend John Elway.

2012 Selected as the number-one NFL draft pick by the Indianapolis Colts; graduates from Stanford University with a degree in architectural design; starts in first NFL game, the Colts' preseason opener against the St. Louis Rams, throwing for 188 yards and 2 touchdowns; sets NFL record for single-game passing yards by a rookie quarterback (433), leading the Colts to a 23-20 win over the Miami Dolphins.

2013 Becomes the first number-one draft pick rookie in NFL history to start a playoff game.

FIND OUT MORE

Books

Fishman, Jon M. *Andrew Luck*. Minneapolis, MN: Lerner, 2013.

Hoblin, Paul. *Andrew Luck: Rising NFL Star*. Minneapolis, MN: Abdo, 2013.

On the Internet

Andrew Luck Fans

http://andrewluckfans.com/

Indianapolis Colts Kids Club

http://www.colts.com/fanzone/clubs/kids-club.html.

Stanford Football

http://bit.ly/15pQ4TP

WTHR.cm: "Andrew Luck's High School Years"

http://www.wthr.com/category/247680/andrew-lucks-high-school-years-slide-show

YouTube: "Touchdown! Shoeless QB"

https://www.youtube.com/watch?v=eq1X6y7PJ9Q

Works Consulted

"Andrew Luck." Biography.com, 2013. http://www.biography.com/people/andrew-luck-20954039

Associated Press. "With a Record Effort, Luck Surrenders Jersey." *The New York Times*, November 7, 2012.

Calabro, Dave. "13 Things You Didn't Know About Andrew Luck." WTHR.com, November 10, 2012.

Chappell, Mike. "Luck, Colts Take First Step in Turning Team Around." *USA Today*, August 12, 2012.

Crossman, Matt. "Andrew Luck: The Next Great Quarterback." *Sporting News*, September 21, 2010.

Dunlevy, Nate. "For a Regular Guy, the Colts' Andrew Luck Is Extraordinary." *BleacherReport.com*, September 4, 2012.

Fitzgerald, Matt. "Grading Andrew Luck's Rookie Season Following Playoff Loss to Ravens." *BleacherReport.com*, January 7, 2013.

Gearhart, Sarah. "Colts Rookie Quarterback Andrew Luck Was a Leader at Stratford High School." *USA Today High School Sports*, December 17, 2012.

King, Peter. "Chuckstrong, Luckstrong." *Sports Illustrated*, December 3, 2012.

MacCambridge, Michael. "Andrew Luck." *Indianapolis Monthly*, October 2, 2012.

Manahan, Kevin. "Andrew Luck's First NFL Throw Is a 63-Yard Touchdown Pass." *USA Today*, August 13, 2012.

Murphy, Austin. "Man with a Plan." *Sports Illustrated*, June 13, 2011.

Peters, Mark. *The Ultimate Andrew Luck Fun Fact and Trivia Book*. Perfect World Marketing, 2013.

Soler, Andrew. *Biography on Andrew Luck*. Hyperink, 2012.

Thamel, Pete. "Standing Out and Blending In at Stanford." *The New York Times*, December 30, 2011.

University of Texas at Austin. "Alumni Focus: Full Circle." *UTLaw Magazine*, January 17, 2012.

GLOSSARY

architecture (ARR-kit-ekt-chur) — The study of designing buildings and spaces.

bowl — A championship game in college football.

charity (CHAIR-it-ee) — An organization that helps people in need.

draft — In football, a selection process where each team picks in turn from a roster of eligible players.

homecoming (HOHM-kuhm-ing) — In football, a home game designated with special celebrations.

prodigy (PROD-i-jee) — A young person who is unusually gifted at a certain skill.

rookie (ROOK-ee) — An athlete playing in his or her first professional season.

sack — In football, to tackle the quarterback before he can throw a pass.

safety (SAFE-tee) — In football, a defensive position played by a good tackler who is a team's last line of defense.

scholarship (SKOL-er-ship) — Award money used to pay for school.

valedictorian (val-ed-ik-TOR-ee-un) — Graduate with the highest grades who delivers a speech at graduation.

INDEX